STENCIL CRAFT

TECHNIQUES FOR
FASHION, ART & HOME

STENCIL CRAFT

TECHNIQUES FOR FASHION, ART & HOME

Margaret Peot

NORTH LIGHT BOOKS
CINCINNATI, OHIO
www.createmixedmedia.com

CONTENTS

01

Stencil Basics

Stencil Supplies -- Traditional Stencils -- Found Stencils -- Building a Stencil Library -- Demonstration: Design an Antiqued Tote Bag

8

02

Stencils for Fashion

Working on Fabric -- Demonstration: Paint a Canvas Apron -- Foil -- Demonstration: Stencil with Foil -- Discharge Paste -- Demonstration: Stencil with Discharge Paste -- Derwent Inktense Blocks -- Demonstration: Design a Day of the Dead Messenger Bag

26

WHAT YOU NEED

Stencil Materials
- clear acetate or frosted or matte Mylar
- found stencil objects such as lace, flowers, twigs, etc.

Brushes
- ½" and 1" brights
- 1" chip brush
- 3" foam brush
- stencil brush

Paints and Inks
- Colorbox Fluid Chalk Petal Point pastel ink pad
- Derwent Inktense Color Blocks
- latex paint (flat white)
- liquid or low-viscosity acrylic paints
- Sharpie markers (thick, fine and extra fine)

Fabrics
- burlap tote bag
- canvas apron
- canvas messenger bag
- fabric pieces
- pillow covers
- tablecloth

Paper
- brown craft paper
- card stock
- computer paper
- medium-weight drawing paper
- stationery paper
- tracing paper

Other
- bone folder
- craft knife
- discharge paste
- foil glue

- foil sheet
- glass panel
- iron
- latex gloves
- masking tape
- Mod Podge Gloss
- natural sponge
- pencils
- Preval sprayer and container
- reference photos
- scissors
- self-healing cutting mat
- Spray Mount
- stencil cutter
- stencil burner
- stencils
- Varathane spray
- waxed paper
- wooden box

LASCAUX
Watercolor and ink on Rives BFK paper
22" × 30" (56cm × 76cm)

6

INTRODUCTION

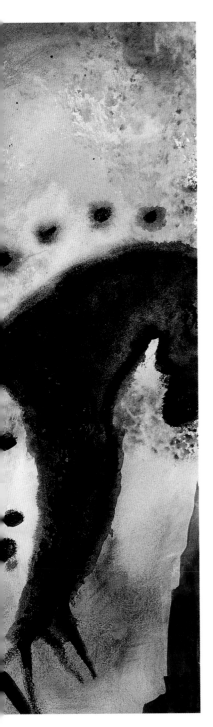

Thousands of years ago deep in a dark cave, a human being put his or her hand on a cave wall and blew paint made with charcoal or mineral powder around it—the first stencil. What was left was the impression of a light hand on the wall surrounded by a vigorous spray of color illuminated by torchlight. The mark looks very immediate—we can almost hear the painter's breath blowing air through a reed to spatter the pigment and water, perhaps just a little further down the tunnel passage.

We don't know why this long-ago artist made a hand stencil. We don't know if it had religious significance or even who made it, whether a man or a woman. We don't know if the makers of the hand stencils were tribal artists who were accorded esteem for their skills, or if they were following the directions of others. We only know that these ancient hand prints exist and that they fill us with curiosity.

All human beings are artists. We all have ideas and pictures in our mind that move and inspire us and we all want to leave our mark on our world. In this book you will make your mark on your world literally—using stencil techniques to paint on clothes, paper and home furnishings for fashion, interior design, art and crafting.

While experimenting with the projects in this book, you will make some beautiful things and some ugly things. You will grow both inspired and frustrated. You will ruin something and throw it away, or a fabulous Phoenix will rise from the ashes, and you will surprise yourself by painting something more fabulous than you ever expected. Just be loose and be flexible so you can respond fluidly to what is in front of you.

Let's get started!

— 7 —

Visit createmixedmedia.com/stencilcraft to access a bonus demonstration.

Acetate and Mylar stencils
for printing creatures, paw
prints, textures and decorative
borders

STENCIL BASICS

A stencil is anything you place on a surface to block paint. You can use stencils to paint specific images, to make textures or to add color. Stencils can be made of almost anything, from carefully cut Mylar to torn brown paper, from masking tape to dried weeds and grasses.

If you tape stripes on a wall and paint the wall, the tape is the stencil. If you hold an oak leaf on a piece of paper and brush paint off the edge of it, the oak leaf is the stencil. If you spray paint onto a surface across a feather or rumpled lace, it can make an almost photographically detailed image. If you scatter a handful of coins across a piece of white fabric and spray aqua fabric paint across them, the coins block the sprayed paint from the fabric and the result is a cheerful dotted fabric that you can make into a summer skirt, or napkins for a picnic.

There are two reasons to use cut stencils, and sometimes they overlap. The main reason to use cut stencils is that you want to print one image more than once—several T-shirts with the same design, an edition of art prints or perhaps signage for a party. The second reason is that you want the particular look that a stencil gives: bold and crisp. In order to function and to be effective, the stencil has to be hyper-designed; highlights and shadows become abstract shapes, lines have changeable weight. Delicate marks are not as easy to get with a stencil. A stencil generally makes marks with a strong appearance and precise edges.

The magic of stencils is that they can be used and reused for a multitude of projects. The same stencil can be used to print a T-shirt, a greeting card, place mats, a tote or can even be worked into a stencil collage.

— **9** —

STENCIL SUPPLIES

A wide variety of plastic, acetate and Mylar can be used for cutting stencils. Some have a low to medium tack adhesive to prevent the stencil from moving around while you are painting. This tack is especially useful for painting on an upright surface such as a wall and for use in airbrushing as the projected paint from an airbrush can puff up the edge of the stencil and cause overspray.

If you cut a stencil from a material that does not have built-in tack, you can use Spray Mount, a repositionable adhesive made by Scotch. It is different than other spray adhesives as it is not permanent but gives a light tack that is perfect for stencils that you intend to use again and again. When you are storing stencils that have been sprayed with Spray Mount, put waxed paper in between the sticky stencils so they won't stick to each other.

When using Spray Mount, follow the manufacturer's safety directions. Because it is flammable, you must not use it around any open flame such as a fireplace or pilot light. Use Spray Mount only in a well-ventilated space. Use a respirator with the proper cartridges as well.

You do not have to use Spray Mount, however. I didn't for years. If I had a particularly floppy or unwieldy stencil, I rolled up little pieces of tape and stuck them under some edges. That was good enough. But Spray Mount is a wonderful tool that we use often when painting costumes and working with very large and complicated stencils.

STENCIL MATERIAL

Any kind of plastic or acetate without a tacky backing can be used for stencils. You can even use the clear plastic on report covers from an office supply store.

In this book I have mostly used Grafix Drafting Film. It is antistatic treated polyester, accepts pencil or ink, and erases fast and clean. It comes in four different thicknesses. I prefer .004" (.1mm) as it is easy to cut but heavy enough to be durable for reuse.

Films made by Grafix Plastics can have one or both sides shiny. These will work if you can't get the two-

CREATING A WORK SPACE

Your work space doesn't have to be elaborate, but ideally, it should not be one you have to clean up before you set the table for dinner! Look around and see if there is a workspace you can call your own. For those of us with space limitations, Ikea sells a table that can hinge out from the wall and then fold down against the wall when you are finished with your projects.

A hollow-core door set up on shelves works well, too. It is nice to have a corkboard to tack up things to look at. Corkboards are also great places to hang stencils to dry. Most of your supplies will fit into a plastic storage bin that can be slid under your worktable.

As far as lighting goes, a window isn't always the best light unless it is from a north-facing window, and sunlight doesn't beam in directly on your work surface. A desk lamp or a couple of clip lights can provide all the light you need.

sided matte. The matte is nice because you can draw on it with a pencil. It's available in roll or sheet form.

Plastic-like without a tacky backing:
- Grafix Clear-Lay Film (Comes in rolls and pads of various sizes.)
- Grafix Drafting Film, .004" (.1mm) Matte
- Grafix Edge Film (Comes in rolls or packs of 9" × 12" [23cm × 30cm] sheets.)

Plastic-like, with a tacky backing:
- Grafix Edge Frisket Film in extra tack and low tack. (Extra tack is good if you are working on a very textural surface such as concrete; low tack is good for work on slick surfaces such as glass or plastic.)
- Original Frisket Film (Comes in rolls or packages of 10" × 15" [25cm × 38cm] sheets; low-tack adhesive masking film.)
- Iwata Art Mask Frisk Film (Comes in rolls; medium tack is great for curved surfaces.)

- Anchor Continental Formula III Signblast Tape (Comes in rolls with low-tack adhesive.)
- Contact paper (Usually a vinyl-like substance printed with faux wood or a design, available at hardware or home stores.)

Paper-based:
- Oil board (Thick posterboard-like material impregnated with dried oil to enhance water resistance.)
- Scratch-Art Wax-O Stencil Paper (Heavy waxed paper available in sheets that resist water and oil-based paints.; translucent and easy to see through.)
- Dot, lozenge-shaped and label stickers as well as masking tape make good stencils.

STENCIL CUTTERS

A variety of implements are available for cutting stencils, from scissors to an electronic stencil-cutting machine. You can use a craft knife or a stencil burner, which melts through stencil plastic with a hot tip much like a fine soldering iron. The implement you

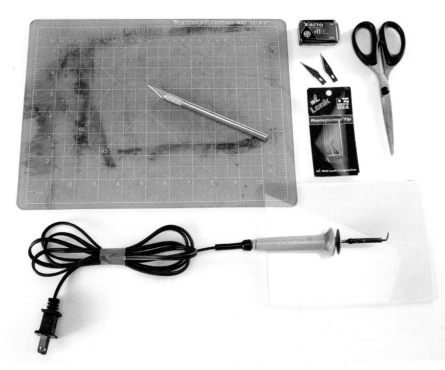

Stencil-Cutting Tools
Scissors, craft knives and stencil burners all work for cutting plastic stencils. If you use oil board or Scratch-Art Wax-O Stencil Paper, you can tear stencils for an interesting textural effect.

— 11 —

choose should depend on both the level of detail you are cutting and the number of stencils you need to cut.

- **Craft knife:** I think the size 11 blade works best for stencil cutting, but some artists prefer a smaller blade. The size 4 blade is better for getting around the curves of intricate stencils.
- **Creative 5-in-1 Tool Kit:** Includes tips for hot-cutting stencils, wood burning and soldering.
- **Walnut Hollow Creative Versa-Tool:** For hot-cutting stencils. Also includes eleven tips for other purposes such as wood burning, soldering, leather crafting and embossing.
- **Silhouette Cameo electronic cutting tool:** This electronic device plugs into your printer, but instead of printing a line drawing, it uses a tiny blade to cut the drawing into different materials such as card stock, stencil vinyl, heat transfer material, etc. This is a very efficient tool if you are cutting a lot of stencils.
- **Scissors:** Great for cutting simple shapes.

STENCIL BURNERS

To cut very intricate designs into stencil Mylar, you can use a stencil burner such as the Creative 5-in-1 or the Walnut Hollow Creative Versa-Tool. Plaid makes a craft stencil cutter, Wall Lenk makes a stencil-cutting pen or stencil cutter. The essence of these tools is the same though: There is a wooden or plastic insulating handle with a metal point in it that heats up when plugged into a regular outlet. The tip heats up enough to melt stencil Mylar or acetate. So while it is called a cutter in most cases, it actually melts the Mylar material. This is why I call it a stencil burner.

When you use a stencil burner, you have to put the stencil material on a surface that is not affected by heat—one that won't melt or char. The best surface is a piece of glass. An added benefit of glass is that you can put a design under clear glass, tape the Mylar on top of it, and be able to see through to your design while you are cutting.

A stencil burner will take a little practice to use. You have to cut at a particular speed—not too fast or the stencil will not cut thoroughly, and not too slow or big beads of plastic can form. These beads are not the end of the world—you can just break them off, but it adds an extra step.

Another benefit to using a stencil burner is that you can cut a lot of stencils—it really saves your hands. Craft knives can be fatiguing when doing a lot of cutting. If you can remind yourself to not press too hard when using a stencil burner, you can glide it around and cut easily.

There is one serious drawback to stencil burners, though. Because they melt the Mylar when they cut through it, the process produces fumes that are toxic. You should always use a stencil burner in a well-ventilated space with a suitable respirator. Also, the tool

Working with Stencil Burners
After you cut a Mylar stencil with a stencil burner, sometimes the stencil will stick a little to the glass where it has melted and attached itself. Be sure to peel the stencil up carefully. You can see here the level of detail you can get with this tool.

gets very hot. Most stencil burning tools come with a metal stand, which will keep the tool from burning your work surface.

BRUSHES

Brushes come in a dizzying array of types and sizes. In art supply stores you will find racks and racks of them—for oils, acrylics, watercolor and multi-purpose. There are synthetic brushes and natural bristle brushes. Some brushes cost less than a dollar, and others cost more than a hundred dollars!

You may already have brushes that you love, but if not, you will eventually find brushes that suit what you want to do exactly. For the projects in this book, you need to have just a small selection of art brushes. If you buy your brushes at a craft supply store, you can sometimes find a selection of brushes packaged together—a couple of round brushes and a couple of flat ones in varying sizes. These are just fine to start with.

At an art supply store the brushes are organized in racks by mediums they are used for. You will want either all-purpose brushes or acrylic brushes that have a medium-soft bristle. All of the different brands of brushes have different numbering systems. Pick two round brushes, one about 1" (25mm), and one about half that size (13mm). Select three bright brushes, one about 1" (25mm), one ½" (13mm), and one ¼" (.7mm). Then get an inexpensive chip brush that is 1 ½" -2"

(38mm–50mm). That will be enough brushes for you to have fun with for some time.

When you buy any brush, make sure the bristles are secure in the ferrule (the metal part of the brush) and that there are no stray bristles sticking out to the side. See that the brush is symmetrical and doesn't have any gaps in the bristles that would make painting frustrating.

We are currently in a culture where natural is considered better. But with brushes, you can have a very high quality useful brush made with man-made fibers that will serve you far better than a natural bristle brush. Buying an expensive badger bristle brush will not necessarily ensure an elegant art-making experience—you just need to have the right brush for what you want to paint.

STENCIL BRUSHES

Stencil brushes are fat round brushes with a blunt end and bristles set tightly together in the ferrule. You can also get flat-ended stencil brushes made of foam. To paint with one, dab a small amount of paint onto the brush and tap off the excess on a piece of paper towel. Then brush off the edges of the stencil onto the paper, or stamp the flat end in a tap-tap-tapping rhythm. When painting with stencils it is most important that you not push paint under the edge of the stencil and that you always brush away from the edge of the stencil towards the middle of the area you are painting. If you follow this, you can use almost any kind of brush.

Assorted Brushes
From left to right: filbert brushes, bright brushes, round brush, chip brush and foam brush—a small selection of the wide world of brushes.

Visit createmixedmedia.com/stencilcraft to access a bonus demonstration.

You do not necessarily need to have a stencil brush to paint over a stencil. True life confession: I did not use a stencil brush for almost twenty-five years of costume painting. I didn't like the ones I had used in the past and felt that I had little control with them. I was fully prepared to tell readers that they could forget about stencil brushes altogether. For the purposes of this book, though, I felt that I needed to at least have a picture of a stencil brush. I bought a high-quality one from Blick Studio and used it once to demo how one might use a stencil brush. I *loved* it! The lesson here is to get a stencil brush with bristles packed tight in the ferrule and a very flat painting surface with no extra bristles sticking out randomly. I got a brush in a mid-price range instead of the least expensive ones.

As an alternative to a brush, you can use a natural or man-made sponge or a sponge brush. You can spray paint through a stencil or even lay a piece of lace on top of your stencil and spray through the lace for an interesting effect.

I have also found good brushes for stenciling in beauty supply stores. Not the fluffy brushes for applying blush, but brushes with denser, slightly stiffer bristles. Makeup brushes are easy to handle and, generally, they are less expensive than brushes sold in art supply stores.

ART-MAKING KIT

You can stencil with a minimal amount of supplies and space. While every project in this book calls for specific materials (fabric paint, for example, or a lightbox), some basic supplies will let you start making a variety of stencils for lots of different projects. If you don't have a designated art-making spot, consider getting a plastic storage box to put supplies in to keep them together and portable—an art-making kit. You may have some of these things already:

- unlined paper (regular computer paper will do)
- stencil material
- pencil
- pencil sharpener
- metal ruler
- Sharpie markers (thick, fine and extra fine)
- small plastic containers with lids
- paper towels
- quart jar or plastic container for water
- scissors
- craft knife with extra blades
- self-healing cutting mat
- newspaper to protect your work surface
- selection of round and bright brushes

Stencil Brushes
The stencil brush has bristles set in a round ferrule (the metal part). The bristles are blunt, making a flat, round end to apply paint. Stencil brushes are also sometimes made of a fat, squat cylinder of foam set in a metal ferrule.

TRADITIONAL STENCILS

The stencils we are most familiar with have a design cut through thin plastic or oil paper. We can paint through them to transfer an image to most surfaces. There are many beautiful pre-cut stencils available at hobby and craft stores—flowers, geometric designs, fleurs de lis, whimsical borders for decorating a wall. Number and letter stencils can be purchased at hardware and office supply stores.

You can also cut your own stencils into Mylar (a thin plastic) or oiled stencil paper. Any image you can think of can be translated to a cut stencil: coral, waves, landscapes, faces, a cityscape, flora and fauna. You can cut a simple silhouette or make a more complicated stencil with interior details by adding bridges to hold the middle of the stencil together.

Positive/Negative Stencils
You can change the look of any drawing depending on how you choose to cut it out. Here are three different flower drawings on tracing paper. The first drawing indicates how the stencil would look if you cut away all of the marked areas, which would leave the flowers white. This is known as a negative stencil; the negative areas being the most important. The second drawing shows how it would look like if you cut out the flowers so that the negative space would be white and the flowers black. This is a positive stencil, as the negative space is minimized and the flowers are the dominant image. The last drawing is a combination of positive and negative stenciling. It is always a good idea to work out a complicated stencil like this on tracing paper first.

Simple Silhouette
The crow on this tote is a good example of a simple silhouette stenciled image. It was attached to the tote with rolled up tape on the back side, then painted around. (Remember to brush off the edge of the stencil and not back towards it!)

The planets are moon drawings by Hevelius and Galileo printed onto heat transfer paper and ironed onto the tote. Black, pearlescent copper and gold acrylic paint were used.

— 15 —

Visit createmixedmedia.com/stencilcraft to access a bonus demonstration.

Stencils With Interior Details

The drawing on the right is a simple silhouette of a bird. The stencil on the left is a bird with interior details. If you want to cut a stencil that has more interior detail you can leave bridges, or connective tabs, that hold the stencil together. In some cases you must plan bridges—if you wanted to make a stencil of the letter R, for example, you would need to have at least one or two tabs to hold the middle of the R in place. In other cases the bridges are not structural but decorative, as in these two bird stencils.

PAINTING "OFF THE EDGE"

No matter how fine the detail in your stencil, you must always make an effort to paint off the edge of the stencil onto your painting surface. When you paint towards a stencil, it will often push paint under the edge of the stencil, blur your image, get paint on the back of the stencil, and generally make a mess. Instead, start your paint-loaded brush on the stencil material itself and brush towards the center of the image. It doesn't really matter what kind of brush you use as long as you brush away from the edge of the stencil. Even if you are spraying a stencil with an airbrush or other sprayer, try not to point the airbrush towards the edge of the stencil. This will help to avoid overspray on the surfaces you have masked out.

FOUND STENCILS

Coins, keys, leaves, weeds and flowers, plastic lizards, snakes and bugs, beads, chains, plastic doodads, nuts, bolts and more can all make wonderful stencils. In the theater sometimes scenic artists scatter sawdust on a surface and spray paint across that to make a rough textured surface. I have used oatmeal for a similar effect on paper and dried spaghetti noodles to emulate shafts of light or rain. Lace and fabric with an open weave, such as erosion cloth or burlap, can be used to spray through to make interesting textures.

So let's explore some found stencils. Compare the different effects you get painting over them with a brush versus a sponge, or spraying acrylic at them with a Preval sprayer. When you start to look at the whole world as a source for stencils, it can make every moment an art-making moment.

Many Different Found Objects Can Be Used as Stencils
As you look around your home and garage, as well as hobby, hardware and fabric stores, you will find lots of things that can be used as stencils. Most things will have to be dedicated forever to the stencil realm if you use acrylic paint, as acrylic paint is permanent.

Visit createmixedmedia.com/stencilcraft to access a bonus demonstration.

NATURAL STENCILS

These are various stencil experiments using found grasses, florist ferns, feathers, geranium cuttings, curled ribbon, pasta and other things. They were done in acrylic, gouache and ink on Rives BFK paper. As you experiment with various found objects, consider using the same color paint; black or maybe a delft blue. The resulting collection of experiments could either make a dramatic quilt top if painted with acrylic on plain white cotton or, if painted on paper, they could be collaged onto a large stretched canvas.

Dried Hydrangea
This abstracted landscape was made by spraying white gouache thinned with water onto a cut Mylar horizon line. Dried hydrangea flowers were used to make the billowing clouds. After the gouache dried, I painted India ink over the whole thing with a foam brush. (This is partly what caused the faint horizontal black lines.) Once dry, I rinsed it in water. The gouache dissolved under the ink, and the picture was revealed.

Receive bonus content when you sign up for our free newsletter at createmixedmedia.com.

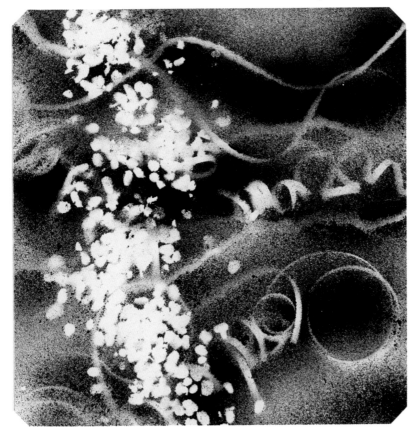

Oatmeal and Curling Ribbon

For this confetti and ribbon image, I secured curling ribbon lightly to paper with a little tape and sprinkled oatmeal. I sprayed black acrylic thinned with water through a pump sprayer (like a plant mister) for a coarse spray texture.

Autumn Leaves

For this leaf pattern, I laid two or three different leaves on the paper and sprayed them with black acrylic thinned with water using a Preval sprayer. While the leaves were still wet with paint, I flipped them and pressed them into the paper in an empty spot, holding the leaf down with one hand while rubbing gently along the veins with my finger.

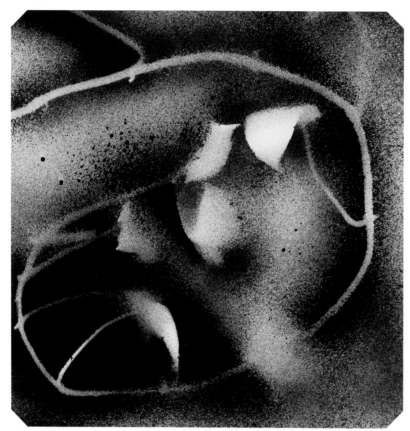

Philodendron Vine
This found object is a cutting from one of my dangling philodendron plants. I coiled it on the paper and sprayed across with black acrylic thinned with water.

Florist Fern
This image was made by spraying white gouache thinned with water across a fern. After the gouache dried, I painted India ink over the whole thing with a foam brush. Once that was dry, I rinsed it in water. The gouache dissolved under the ink, and the picture was revealed.

Pine Branches
Similar to the fern on the previous page, this wintry image was made by a gouache resist and ink technique.

Sunflowers
These sunflowers with their hanging heads were made by spraying them with black acrylic thinned with water. (This image that would be fun to draw back into with colored pencils or pastels.)

BUILDING A STENCIL LIBRARY

Once you have cut a stencil or set of stencils, they can be used over and over for many different applications. You can use the same stencil to print a greeting card or a T-shirt, decorate gift wrap or use in an amalgam artwork. So it is a good idea to hold on to all of them. Yet stencils, especially ones with tiny interior detail, can be rather delicate and can get easily torn or bent.

After you have cut several stencils, you will want to have a way to store them so the stencils will be safe from harm and so that you can find a stencil or set of stencils at a moments notice.

Stencils are best stored flat. And if you have used Spray Mount on them, they must be stored flat with waxed paper in between the stencils so they don't stick to each other. A flat file with its many shallow drawers is perfect for storing stencils, but not everyone has room for a big set of flat files. Another more economical way to store stencils is to purchase a large newsprint drawing pad—one that is ideally wider and longer than your biggest stencil. You can interleave your stencils in the pages of this newsprint pad, with Post-it Note tabs indicating which sets of stencils are where in the pad. You'll still have to put waxed paper on the sticky side of the stencils you sprayed with Spray Mount, but then they can be stored easily in the newsprint pad as well.

Storing Stencils
Stencils are best stored flat. They can be used again and again for multiple applications in various projects.

CLEANING STENCILS

Mylar stencils can be cleaned in different ways. If you are using acrylic paint, you can wipe off the excess. As long as you haven't left any globs of paint along the edge of your design, you can reuse the stencil with any paint as the dried acrylic won't come off or transfer to the next painting project. You can also wash Mylar stencils with warm soapy water and a kitchen sponge to carefully remove almost all of the paint. Some paint will leave a stain, but that won't negatively affect the usefulness of your stencil. If the paint has dried a little before you wash it, sometimes a sponge that has a scrubby side can be used to coax dried acrylic off in warm soapy water. Many of the stencils in this book have dried paint on them. If you have diligently painted off the edge of your stencils and not back towards them, excess paint won't accumulate on the edges and a little dried paint won't hurt anything.

DESIGN AN ANTIQUED TOTE BAG

This plain tote makes a nice canvas for found object stencils, and the brown acrylic spray on the creamy natural canvas color lends this an antiqued look.

When you use found objects as stencils, their dimensions can sometimes make them tricky to paint onto to make a crisp image. Use masking tape to hold light things, such as grasses or silk flowers, in place so painting into them won't move them around. And if you use spray paint, spray towards the found objects secured to the painting surface from one direction only. If you spray in more than one direction, especially on thin stems and delicate objects, you can make the edges indistinct, and the image will be hard to read when you lift the stencil. If you can spray from one side, found object stencils can make an almost photographic look.

Let found objects dry a bit before lifting them off your painting surface so paint doesn't drip off onto your work.

MATERIALS

canvas tote bag

computer paper

liquid or low-viscosity acrylic paint (Burnt Sienna and Yellow Ochre)

masking tape

natural or artificial flowers, leaves and twigs

Preval sprayer with jar

scissors

scrap of lace

self-healing cutting mat

Sharpie marker (fine point)

Spray Mount

water

waxed paper

In a well-ventilated space, place the tote on a work surface protected with newspaper. Cover the straps with paper secured with tape to keep them clean. Lay your lace scrap on top of the tote. (This tote had a big pocket on one side. I taped two pieces of computer paper together to completely mask the pocket.) Fill the Preval sprayer jar to the halfway point with water. Add about a teaspoon each of the two acrylic colors. Shake it to thoroughly mix the paint. Spray through the lace onto the tote.

Visit createmixedmedia.com/stencilcraft to access a bonus demonstration.

2

Let it dry a little, then lift the lace and put it aside. Lift the paper pocket mask and discard.

I like to pin the lace to the side of my table so it dries crunchy and flat. The more acrylic you spray on lace or net stencils, the more durable they get. You can also wash them by themselves in a washing machine after they dry. The color won't go away, but they will get softer.

3

Tape a 1" (2.5cm) border neatly within the edge of the pocket with masking tape. Then mask off the rest of the bag with masking tape and waxed paper. Arrange the found greenery and secure the pieces with tape.

Spray the tote through the greenery, making sure to spray from the same direction to get a distinct image. Let it dry completely, then lift the greenery, tape and waxed paper.

SAFETY CONCERNS

The sprayed examples I have shown in this book are made with either thinned acrylic or thinned gouache. These paints are relatively non-toxic and have no odor. The exceptions are Cadmiums and Cobalts, which should never be sprayed and should always be used with gloves and caution. I do not recommend using Krylon or other spray paints that contain acetone or toluene.

When you spray any paint, even if it is water-based, you need to use a respirator to avoid inhaling it. You can find respirators suitable for use with paint in hardware stores and online. Ask vendors and read the descriptions carefully to make sure you get exactly what you need— and learn how to use it properly. Always spray in a well-ventilated area.

The Finished Tote

Visit createmixedmedia.com/stencilcraft to access a bonus demonstration.

FOUR-PLY SILK CHARMEUSE
Painted sample with heat-
transferred foil accents
30" × 36" (76cm × 91cm)

STENCILS FOR FASHION

Stencils lend themselves wonderfully to printing on fabric and especially for clothing. For every ten projects I paint at the costume shop, I would say at least eight of them use stencils of some sort—including tape and sticker dots, lace or net to spray through, as well as elaborately cut stencils.

Stencils have long been used for fabric and fashion from Indian textiles, African mud cloth and textiles for the theater to simple stenciling of identifying marks on military clothing.

Once you start stenciling fabric for clothing and accessories, you will begin to see all the possibilities there are. You can give new life to old clothes with delicately stenciled designs or bold logos, or you can personalize a favorite denim jacket or pair of shoes.

Stenciled Wedding Dress

I had the happy opportunity to paint a wedding dress for a good friend. It was a once-in-a-lifetime chance to show how I felt about the bride and groom and their marriage. And it didn't hurt that she wanted a red dress, not a white one, so it could stand some dramatic painting. All the images in the dress--the leaves, the lavender, the cicadas and the scrolls—were from reference the bride gave me and were cut out of Mylar stencils. The design repeated loosely around the hem of the dress.

— 27 —

WORKING ON FABRIC

The two fabric painting samples that head this chapter are painted with the dye-suspended-in-thickener paint that we use to paint costumes for Broadway shows, circuses, ice shows and other arena events. The painted fabric is heat set in a steamer for an hour or more. However, the paints that we use are not available for retail consumption—they are strictly to-the-trade.

If you are painting garments for yourself and others, the paints you use will not have to hold up to the same washing rigors as costumes for theatrical productions would. Happily though, the paints that I have tested for home use do hold up to well. They have a pretty nice hand, which means they don't feel too stiff and crunchy after they are processed according to manufacturer's instructions.

I tested Liquitex acrylic ink colors on this sample but did not test regular acrylics. But I have used acrylics on fabric for years for various projects and feel confident that they will last on almost anything you put them on. In fact, my old cotton canvas work apron has

rotted around all the acrylic on it, and the acrylic is as bright and fresh as the day I wiped it on my apron. You can use acrylics to paint directly on most sturdy fabrics like cotton knit, cotton canvas, muslin and burlap.

The acrylics by themselves do not need to be heat set like many fabric paints do, and will mostly have a rather stiff hand. Liquitex Acrylics and liquid acrylics such as those made by Golden Artist Colors will have a less stiff hand. Liquitex acrylics even state on their packaging that they can be used for fabric painting. Golden Artist Colors makes a medium additive called GAC 900 Fabric Medium that can be added to any of their acrylic products that, when heat set according to the manufacturer's instructions, offers a softer hand and even better wash-fastness than the acrylics by themselves. This additive can be used with any of their acrylic products and can be screen printed, airbrushed or stenciled.

SILK CHIFFON, PAINTED SAMPLE
30" × 42" (76cm × 107cm)

Painting "White"
Painting the red wedding dress got me thinking about how one could paint a wedding dress but still have it appear white overall. As an experiment, I painted this white-on-white (actually pale blues and grays, and a couple of golden lines worked in) chiffon fabric sample. I used stencils to mask out the dragons and mandala motifs, and sprayed the pale gray ombré. Then I took the stencils off and used another stencil to paint the scales.

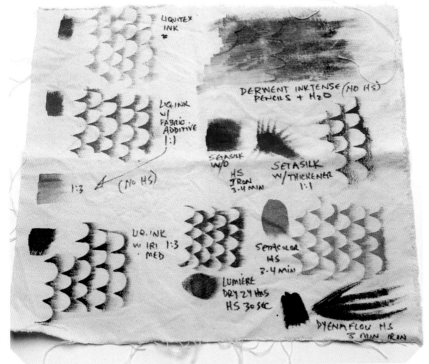

Various Paints on Fabric

This piece of cotton canvas and the silk scarf below were painted with Liquitex ink and a fabric painting additive (both plain and iridescent) made for the same line, Derwent Inktense Blocks, Setasilk fabric paint, Dy-na-Flow and Lumiere Fabric Paint. For the paints that required heat setting (Setasilk, Lumiere and Dy-na-Flow), I did so for the length of time suggested by each manufacturer. I did not heat set any paints where heat setting was not recommended by the manufacturers (Liquitex ink and Derwent Inktense Blocks). I washed these samples ten times in a regular home washing machine in cold water with soap.

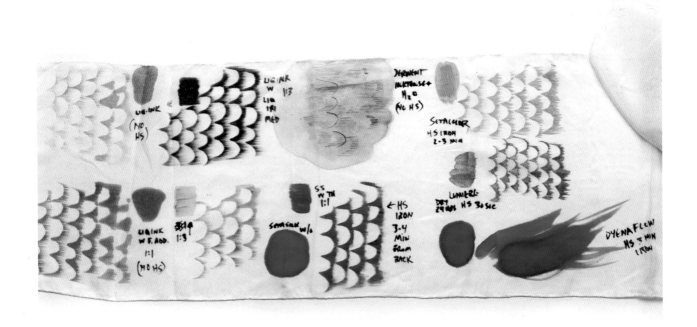

Visit createmixedmedia.com/stencilcraft to access a bonus demonstration.

Einstein Tote, Acrylic on Canvas

A tote makes a wonderful canvas for your new stenciling skills. You can buy blank totes that come ready to dye or paint from many craft stores. Canvas totes are inexpensive, so you could buy several and print totes as fund-raiser gifts for a good cause.

You can dye canvas bags with household dye (available from grocery and sometimes hardware stores) first if you wish, or stencil directly on the natural canvas with acrylic paint.

Paisley Tote, Acrylic, Embroidery Thread and Buttons on Burlap

I used a giant paisley stencil much like this one as a stencil on a pair of pants for the Broadway musical *Aladdin*. Using a gigantic design like this and letting it continue off the edges of the tote gives the piece an exuberant quality. I like these burlap totes from Dharma Trading as they come in this gigantic size into which I can put a portfolio or a big sketch pad.

Octo T-Shirt, Acrylic on Cotton

For this Octo shirt, I used Golden's Titan Buff liquid acrylic paint, placing and painting one tentacle at a time. I painted one coat of buff and let it dry, then painted a second coat to fully cover the black of the shirt. When the second coat of paint was dry, I lifted the sticker dots and the tentacle stencil and placed the second stencil.

The tentacles continue all around the neck of the shirt for a total of eight. It might be fun to design an octopus head stencil and print it on the hood of a sweatshirt, then print eight tentacles all around the neck so that the wearer would appear to be an octopus!

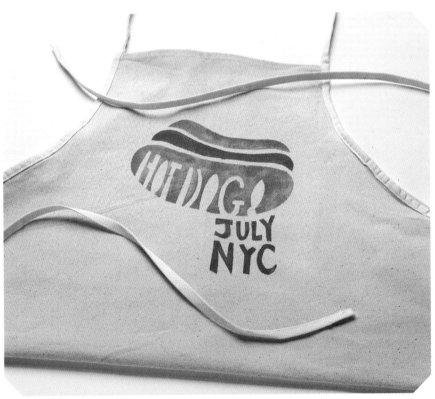

Cookout Apron, Acrylic on Canvas

The inspiration for this project came from my good friend Sue Seitner, who prints funny aprons for her annual family hot dog roast. Everyone in the family can have an apron as most craft stores carry blank aprons in adult and children's sizes.

Remember to always paint away from the stencil and towards the fabric. Because this can get kind of fiddly around the thin letters you see here, use the tip of your brush in a kind of tapping motion, up and down, to avoid getting paint under the edge of the stencil.

Even though this hot dog design is multicolored, I didn't have to cut a different stencil for every color. I used Yellow Ochre for the bun and mixed some pink and red together to get a good hot dog color.

PAINT A CANVAS APRON

A canvas apron is great to print on because it is sturdy and stable. It won't wiggle around while you are trying to get color on it the way a silk scarf can. Acrylics, our paint of choice for canvas, look great on this surface.

When you design your stencils, (in this case, sunflowers) make sure they fit the smallest apron you are going to print unless you are planning to create more than one set of stencils for various sizes of garments.

MATERIALS

acrylic or fabric paint

canvas apron

computer paper

craft knife, stencil burner or scissors (depending on the complexity of your design)

foam brush

frosted or matte Mylar or clear acetate

pencil

masking tape

natural sponge

Sharpie marker (fine point)

Spray Mount

stencil brush

tracing paper

Design the apron. Sketch sunflowers on paper and arrange them on the apron to decide where the flowers should be placed and how big the stencils should be.

2

Place the stencil Mylar over your drawing and trace over the drawing to create your stencil. The simplicity of these flowers lent themselves perfectly to being cut out with scissors. Use Spray Mount on the back of your stencils to keep them in place while painting.

3

Use masking tape to tape off the stem of the flower growing up from the hem.

Visit createmixedmedia.com/stencilcraft to access a bonus demonstration.

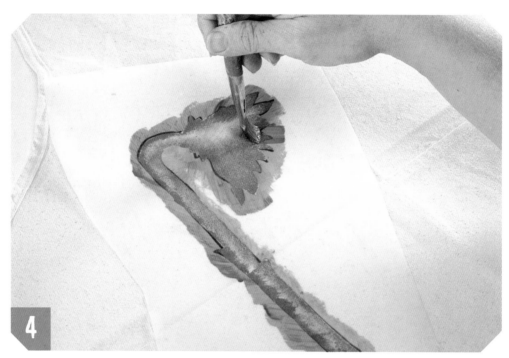

4

Paint the stem and flower back with a stencil brush. I mixed Lumiere Pearl Turquoise and Metallic Gold Light in two different proportions to make warm green and cool green mixtures. You can use acrylic instead. (If you use the Lumiere paint, heat set according to the instructions on the jar.) Leave a small section unpainted for highlight. When painting over a stencil, make sure you paint away from it rather than towards it. You will get a cleaner line when you lift up the stencil.

5

Place the petal stencil and paint with yellow and gold. (I used a primary yellow fabric paint and Lumiere Metallic Gold Light) Then carefully peel off the tape and stencil.

6

Adhere the petal stencil to the apron and paint the gold
for the flower. Then carefully peel back the stencil to
reveal the petal shape.

7

Adhere the other sunflower stencils to the apron and
paint the petals, leaving the center of the flowers
unpainted for now.

Visit createmixedmedia.com/stencilcraft to access a bonus demonstration.

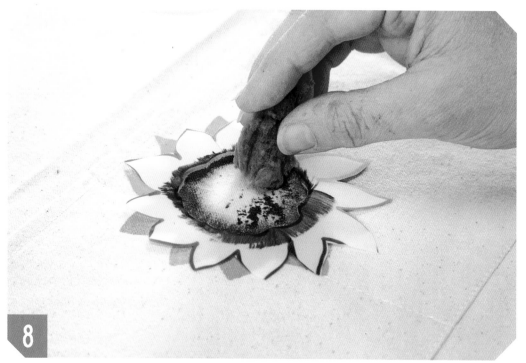

8 Use the cutout flower stencil to cover the petals and begin painting the middle of the flowers. (I used Raw Umber acrylic.) Paint the edge with a brush but then finish coloring the middle with a natural sponge to add texture. Repeat for both flowers.

9 Tape off the stems for the remaining flowers, then add paint. Peel off the masking tape to reveal the stems.

The Finished Apron

Visit createmixedmedia.com/stencilcraft to access a bonus demonstration.

FOIL

Foil is a neat effect, and it works on almost every surface (like on the burlap Octo-tote and the silk velvet pictured below). There are two types of foil glue; one requires heat setting with an iron or a heat-transfer machine, and the other is pressure sensitive. I have used both and have been really enjoying the Jones Tones foil glue. It is the pressure-sensitive kind, which seems to work more reliably than the heat setting kind, especially for home use.

At the costume shop we have a heat-transfer machine that allows us to put a great deal of pressure and heat on a large area of fabric, so it's fabulous for heat setting. It is very difficult to get the same effect with an iron because the heat and pressure is uneven.

To use the pressure-sensitive foil glue, you can either draw with it through the drawing tip included with the glue bottle or squeeze it out and paint or sponge it through a stencil onto your surface. Wait for the glue to dry completely and clear. It will still be sticky but no longer white. Lay the foil color or metallic side up and rub it over the glue. I have found that a bone folder works great for this.

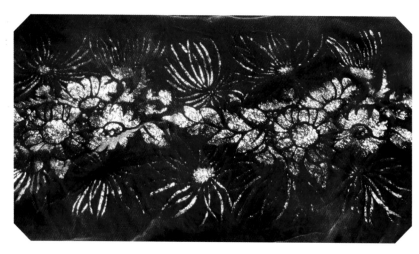

Silk-Rayon Velvet, Stencil Printed With Foil and Foil Glue

Foil glue can be a fun and surprising accent on a plain fabric, or it can be used on a sumptuous fabric, such as this velvet, to make a border on a garment. This border was printed with heat-transfer glue, mashed in a heat-transfer machine, and then washed in cold water so the nap of the velvet would fluff back up.

Octo Tote, Acrylic and Foil on Burlap

These giant octopus tentacles were painted with a Mylar stencil and black acrylic. The circle suckers are Avery sticker dots, which were placed after the stencils were composed on the bag in preparation for painting. The shiny foil contrasts nicely with the roughness of the burlap.

STENCIL WITH FOIL

Follow the steps to enhance your fabric designs with foil stenciling. This dramatic border could be used for curtains, customized bedding or a tablecloth.

MATERIALS

bone folder

craft knife, stencil burner or scissors (depending on the complexity of your design)

foil sheet

frosted or matte Mylar or clear acetate

Jones Tones foil glue

liquid or low viscosity acrylic paint

masking tape

pencil

piece of fabric

self-healing cutting mat

Sharpie marker (fine point)

stencil brush

tracing paper

1 Tape out a border. I made mine 2" (5cm). Use the stencil itself as a registering guide as you place and paint the design. Measure and make light pencil marks on the fabric to guide where the next row of stencils will go.

The two shades of purple I used add richness and interest to the open stencil areas.

2 Lay a piece of tracing paper over the printed fabric to design the stencil with which you will apply foil to embellish the design. The foil stencil should complement the original stencil design.

— 39 —

3 Apply foil glue with a stencil brush and allow it to dry. It will appear clear and feel tacky. Wash the brush right away!

WASHING FOIL GLUE

Foil glue cannot be dry-cleaned and must be washed with a delicate hand. This is such a gorgeous effect, but perhaps a bit impractical for garments that require frequent washing. It can be used to good effect on things that don't get washed or dry-cleaned, however, such as some craft pieces, props, hats, etc. It works well for items in the home that can be handwashed and hung to dry. You can even touch it up yourself when it starts to look worn and less shiny.

4 Place a foil sheet onto the glue with the metallic side up and use a bone folder to rub where there is glue.

Peel back the foil sheet to reveal the finished design.

The Finished Piece

Visit createmixedmedia.com/stencilcraft to access a bonus demonstration.

DISCHARGE PASTE

Jacquard makes a discharge paste color remover (available from Dharma Trading) that is safe to use on most natural fibers including silk. It is approximately the thickness and consistency of yogurt and can be used for painting and stencil printing, even silk screening. After the paste is dry, you heat it by ironing or steaming to remove the color. Many home-dyed fabrics will discharge easily, and lots of different purchased fabrics do as well.

A word of caution: Don't use your best iron for this! I have an iron I use exclusively for crafts, heat-setting paint, using heat transfers, adhering foil and using discharge paste. You can also steam fabric painted with discharge paste in a steamer if you are set up to do this.

Before you get really invested in a big stencil project, it is always best to test a bit of fabric before you do the whole thing. For a piece of fabric, just cut a bit off and test it. On a garment you can find a tiny place inside the garment, such as a small seam allowance, where you can do a test.

Sometimes the lighter color you end up with is surprising. Blacks will sometimes discharge to a pale gray, but more often than not will remove to a gorgeous golden brown or reddish brown. In one disappointing case, I removed an elaborate border on a skirt without testing an inside corner first. I painted on the discharge paste, let it dry and ironed the border. The color appeared to remove to a lovely silvery gray. I popped the skirt in the washer to wash out the excess paste, but when it came out, there was absolutely no sign of color coming out of the fabric at all!

Jacquard Discharge Paste Color Remover on Cotton
Discharge paste is safe on cotton, rayon and some silks, but remember— it's always best to test a little corner first before diving into a whole project. Even on garments, you should try to find a little internal seam allowance to test. This cotton-ribbed tank top was an excellent surface to discharge this deer head. It color-removed to an appealing golden-brown color.

CLEANING YOUR IRON

My fiber art teacher in college taught me a great method for cleaning a home iron. Plug in the iron and heat it to its hottest setting. Put a large brown paper grocery bag on your ironing board, and put two or three tablespoons of table salt on the bag. When the iron is hot, iron the salt on the bag with some pressure. The heat softens whatever goo is on the iron, and the salt scrubs it off. Then fold up the bag with the salt inside and discard. You can use this method to clean any iron. Sometimes even if an iron appears to be super clean, it isn't, so I clean my iron before and after projects. This can save a lot of grief!

STENCIL WITH DISCHARGE PASTE

Follow the steps to learn how to stencil using discharge paste color remover. Always be sure to read the manufacturer's safety instructions before using discharge paste.

MATERIALS

dark piece of fabric

discharge paste

iron

stencil

stencil brush

Lay your stencil onto a dark piece of fabric. Brush discharge paste over the stencil with a stencil brush. Allow it to dry thoroughly.

Iron the printed area with a heat setting appropriate for your fabric. Watch the color magically disappear! Then machine wash the piece in cold water to remove any excess paste.

Visit createmixedmedia.com/stencilcraft to access a bonus demonstration.

DERWENT INKTENSE BLOCKS

Derwent makes ink blocks and pencils that are water soluble on application but waterproof once dry. You can draw with them on any surface and then wet the drawing with a brush for a watercolor effect, much like a watercolor pencil. This has wonderful applications for fabric painting as there are no other fabric-painting tools or substances that can give the effect of a vigorous, roughly drawn mark. The very rough and active mark of these blocks looks great when used with a stencil. The stencil gives the rather granular mark a neat edge, and the texture gives the stencil a

new life. The marks they make on fabric do not need to be heat set and hold up well to multiple washings.

To use the Derwent Blocks on fabric, dip the end in water before applying it to the fabric. After you have completed your drawing on the fabric, you will need to machine wash it to get the excess crumbs of the ink stick off. Wash the fabric by itself in cold water so it has room to move around.

Derwent also makes a holder for the blocks, as the permanent ink can stain your hands. In lieu of the block holder, wear gloves to protect your hands.

Derwent Inktense Blocks on Silk Broadcloth
This scarf square uses the positive of the deer stencil from the Discharge Paste example. The very painterly textural mark of the Inktense Blocks changes the look of the stencil.

DESIGN A DAY OF THE DEAD MESSENGER BAG

Damien Hirst and Alexander McQueen have made the skull stylish. This Day of the Dead messenger bag is a funky way to carry your sketchbook and supplies to art class.

MATERIALS

1" (25mm) bright brush

canvas messenger bag

craft knife, stencil burner or scissors (depending on the complexity of your design)

Derwent Inktense Blocks

frosted or matte Mylar or clear acetate

pencil

latex gloves

masking tape

medium-weight drawing paper

self-healing cutting mat

Sharpie marker (fine point)

water

1

Sketch out a loose design for your Day of the Dead skull, making sure it fits nicely on the messenger bag.

Visit createmixedmedia.com/stencilcraft to access a bonus demonstration.

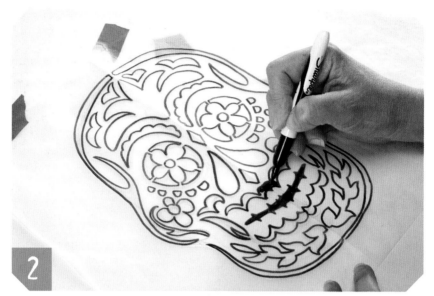

2

Lay a piece of stencil Mylar over the drawing and refine your design with a Sharpie marker. Cut out the design with a craft knife or a stencil burner.

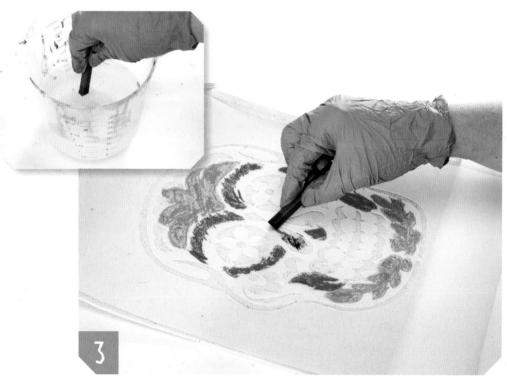

3

Using the colors of your choice, dip the tip of the Inktense sticks into water before applying them over the stencil. As you apply the Inktense sticks, color off the edges of the stencil in a chunky slightly sloppy way. While the color is still wet, go over it with a 1" (25mm) bright brush to create a watercolor effect.

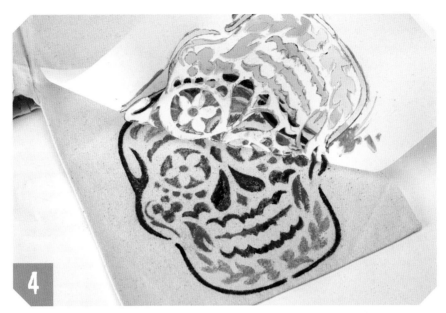

4

Once all your color has been applied, carefully peel back the stencil to reveal the finished design. Machine wash the bag separately in cold water to set the color and remove any excess flakes from the Inktense sticks.

The Finished Tote Bag

Visit createmixedmedia.com/stencilcraft to access a bonus demonstration.

STENCILS FOR HOME

03

Stencils have been used for painting on walls, floors and furniture for centuries. You can enliven a plain wall with a riot of blossoms or an austere and elegant border. Rescue a street-find table with a faux inlaid tile design, huge sunflowers, or maybe animals and the alphabet for a children's drawing table. Some quilters stencil fabrics to incorporate into their pieced designs, or stencil on top of quilted pieces to unify their images. Onboard an eighteenth-century sailing ship, the captain might decorate his cabin with a stenciled checkered design on a piece of sailcloth—the precursor to modern linoleum.

There are hundreds of things to stencil for the home. You can stencil the alphabet, a farmyard or an airport on a child's wall, or silvery wheat grasses, an elegant brocade, subtle stripes or a gorgeous flower garden in a bedroom or family room. You can give new life to old furniture with stencils or personalize wooden serving trays, frames and cork bulletin boards.

In this chapter we will explore painting soft goods such as a tablecloth for a blue-and-white tea party, and pastel cupcakes on decorative throw pillow covers. We will paint a small wooden treasure box with a fool-the-eye tile design and explore repeating patterns by painting a small floor mat for a high-use area. I have just scratched the surface here but I hope these projects will give you some good ideas.

— **49** —

DINING ROOM

Stencils give these plain white table linens a cheerful look. You can buy new white tablecloths and napkins to decorate or use stencils to creatively disguise a stained tablecloth. A scattering of stenciled blossoms and rose petals could give new life to a splashed or spattered tablecloth.

Blue Plate Special
Tablecloths, napkins, place mats and runners are the perfect canvas on which to show off your stenciling skills. One winter I printed tons of tea towels and ended up selling them all at a pop-up holiday sale.

Presentation and Protection
I fold each tea towel I print for sale and slip it into an acetate envelope. I leave only one out for prospective customers to look at and touch. Not only does this give them a nice professional look for gift giving, it also protects the pristine white towels from getting soiled before they've sold.

PRINT A TABLECLOTH

Follow the steps to stencil and print your own unique tablecloths, tea towels and napkins. For this project we'll go with a tea party theme.

MATERIALS

computer paper

craft knife, stencil burner or scissors (depending on the complexity of your design)

frosted or matte Mylar or clear acetate

liquid or low-viscosity acrylic paint (warm and cool blue)

pencil

self-healing cutting mat

Sharpie markers (thick and fine-point)

Spray Mount

stencil brush

tablecloth

tracing paper

Sketch your stencil design onto computer paper with a pencil.

Visit createmixedmedia.com/stencilcraft to access a bonus demonstration.

2

Refine your sketch and fill in the design with a thick
Sharpie marker.

3

Lay a sheet of matte Mylar over the inked sketch. Do a
line drawing over the sketch with a fine-point Sharpie.
The Sharpie line is permanent and won't transfer to your
fabric when you are painting.

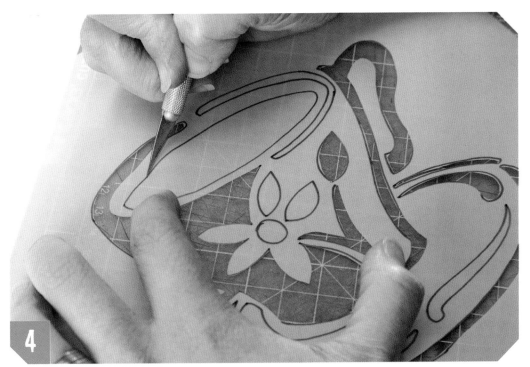

4

Cut out the stencil with a craft knife. (For some of the smaller more detailed areas, you may wish to use a stencil burner.)

5

Apply Spray Mount to the back of the stencil. Lightly affix the stencil to the fabric. Using the stencil brush, lightly tap the paint onto the fabric through the stencil.

Visit createmixedmedia.com/stencilcraft to access a bonus demonstration.

6

Continue painting through the stencil, using both blues. You can paint lightly in some places and heavier in others to vary the texture and add interest.

7

Carefully peel off the stencil to reveal the finished design.

The Finished Tablecloth

Visit createmixedmedia.com/stencilcraft to access a bonus demonstration.

BEDROOM

Add new life to tired throw pillows by decorating simple canvas or cotton pillow covers with stencils. Pillow covers complete with zippers are available from Dharma Trading and come dye and print ready.

You could stencil your monogram, a "Keep Calm" message, billowy clouds or birds for your napping and dreaming couch—the possibilities are endless.. You can also print borders on the doubled-over open edge of pillowcases for a pretty, creative gift idea.

Dye and Acrylic on Silk Broadcloth
This silk broadcloth was spattered with thinned dye paint to give a variegated background to abstracted leaves and flourishes printed with acrylic.

Textile Paint and Acrylic on Brocade
Brocade remnants make interesting surfaces to stencil on—the pattern comes and goes under the stencil design. Leafy branch stencils and Avery sticker dots were sprayed with Burnt Umber acrylic and water in a Preval sprayer. Gold metallic dots were added with Jacquard Lumiere Bright Gold textile paint.

Acrylic on Denim
This pillow was printed with three stencils inspired by ikat weaving. I used a palette onto which I mixed four different greens with Golden Fluid Acrylics—Titan Buff, Hansa Yellow Medium, Sap Green Hue, Phthalo Green and Raw Sienna—and applied the paint with a natural sponge.

Acrylic on Brocade
Brocade that already has a grid pattern makes stenciling a symmetrical pattern a snap. I sponged on two blue-greens, being careful to hit all of the edges that defined the pattern, but I left some gold peeking through within the design so this giant stencil would not look too heavy.

PRINT PILLOW COVERS

Follow the steps to stencil and print your own unique pillow covers. You can purchase plain decorative pillow covers at a home goods store. They are also available through Dharma Trading.

MATERIALS

craft knife, stencil burner or scissors (depending on the complexity of your design)

frosted or matte Mylar or clear acetate

liquid or low-viscosity acrylic paint

masking tape

medium-weight drawing paper

pencil

plain pillow cover

self-healing cutting mat

Sharpie markers (thick and fine-point)

Spray Mount

stencil brush

waxed paper

water

1

Sketch your stencil design onto medium-weight drawing paper with a pencil.

Visit createmixedmedia.com/stencilcraft to access a bonus demonstration.

2

Fill in the stencil with a thick Sharpie marker.

3

Lay a sheet of frosted or matte Mylar (or clear acetate) over the inked sketch. Do a line drawing over the sketch with a fine-point Sharpie. Cut out the stencil. At this point you will want to cut all your stencils for multiple layering. (More on multiple layering in Step 6.)

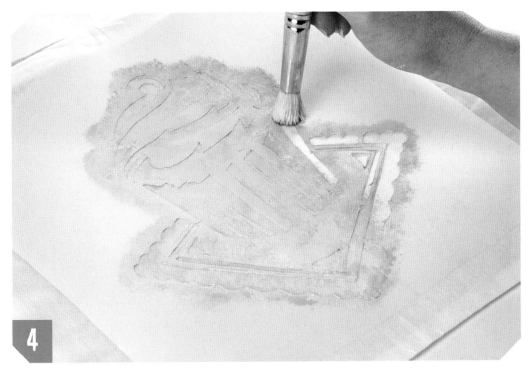

4

Place waxed paper inside the pillow cover to keep the layers from sticking together when you apply the paint. Apply Spray Mount to the back of the stencil. Lightly affix the stencil to the fabric. Using a stencil brush, lightly tap paint onto the fabric through the stencil.

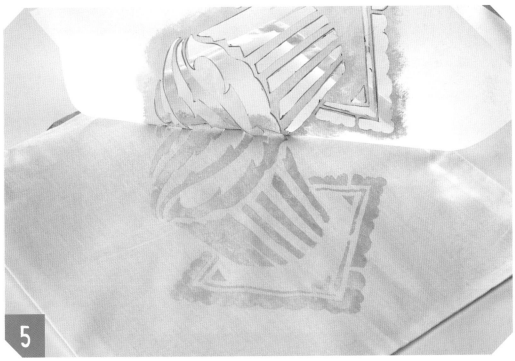

5

Allow the first layer to dry, then carefully peel back the stencil.

6

Add another stencil layer. (In this case it stops the pale yellow from getting lost on the white.) After the first layer is dry, tape a piece of Mylar over the image and trace it with a fine-point Sharpie where you want the next paint color to go. Apply Spray Mount to the back of the stencil, affix the stencil to the fabric and paint onto the fabric through the stencil.

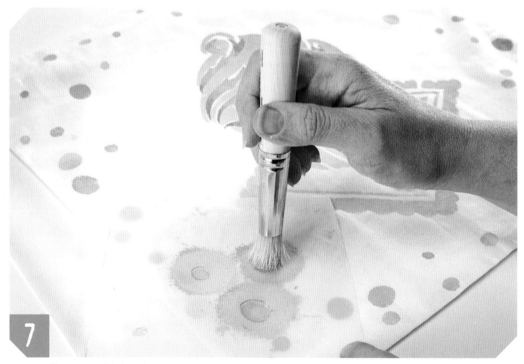

7

You can add details and embellish the design to improve it as you go along. Here I added confetti-like dots through a simple stencil.

FINISHED PILLOW COVERS

Visit createmixedmedia.com/stencilcraft to access a bonus demonstration.

FLOOR CLOTHS AND MATS

In the times of sailing ships sailcloth manufacturers made huge canvas, which was perfect for covering the floor on board ship. The floor of the captain's wide and airy cabin might have been covered with a canvas decorated with a black-and-white checkered pattern. Sailcloth was also used in drawing rooms on dry land. This might have been the precursor to linoleum.

To make a floor cloth, prime the back of a stapled-down canvas with a 1:1 mixture of poly-vinyl acetate glue and water. Let it dry. Flip the canvas and prime it again. Trim and turn the edges under, then glue them. Prime with paint, then paint the design and seal with several coats of sealer.

I have found, however, that you can eliminate a lot of these steps by painting your design on the back of a piece of rolled linoleum from a flooring store. Linoleum is usually twelve feet wide and sold by the foot. If the piece you want to paint is small enough, though, a flooring company might have a scrap they can give you for free. They often have stacks and rolls of pieces from installation jobs that are too big to throw away and too small to sell.

Linoleum is printed with a wide variety of patterns, which you can ignore, as that will be the side facing the floor. The important thing is to choose a linoleum with a white absorbent backing (it feels a little bit like soft felt) rather than a slick backing. The slick stuff will not work for this type of project.

Kitchen Floor Cloth
This design was painted with acrylic. I knew that I had a limited amount of time to paint this floor cloth and little chance of making the tiny tiles come out perfectly, so I built imperfection into the design. You can see that the tiles are sometimes "laid" crookedly. Because this floor cloth was in a very high-traffic area, I applied four coats of Varathane (a water based polyurethane-like sealer) to the finished design and waited three days before walking on it.

DESIGN A FLOOR MAT

A textural, tiled floor mat like this one, if coated with three or more coats of sealer, can be used to protect a high-traffic area in your home. The texture will hide any scuffs or discoloration.

After you are finished painting your floor mat, seal it with at least three coats of clear Varathane to protect it. And because the other side of the linoleum is slick, you must use a rubberized, non-slip rug mat underneath to prevent it from sliding.

This floor mat is a stone tile design. The dimensions of the tiles were made by first printing a dark version of the stencil, then shifting the stencil slightly and printing a lighter version on top, a trick often used by theatrical scenic artists.

MATERIALS

3" (75mm) foam brush

acrylic paint (Burnt Sienna, Phthalo and Yellow Ochre)

brown craft paper

craft knife, stencil burner or scissors (depending on the complexity of your design)

frosted or matte Mylar or clear acetate

glass panel

latex paint (flat white)

linoleum

masking tape

natural sponge

pencil

Sharpie marker (thick)

Spray Mount

Styrofoam plates

Varathane spray

wooden craft sticks

1 Cut the linoleum to the size you would like your floor mat to be. Cut brown craft paper to the same size as the floor mat. Fold the paper in quarters and then eighths to give yourself a guide for designing the shape and sizes of your tiles. Sketch your tile designs with a pencil. Then commit to the final design with a thick Sharpie marker.

2

Secure a piece of glass over your sketched design with masking tape. Tape down the stencil Mylar over the glass. Once your stencil burner is hot, trace over your design lines to cut the shapes out of the Mylar. Cut out all of your stencils. If you go too quickly, the stencil burner can't cut all the way through, so take your time. When cutting your lines don't worry about getting things perfectly straight. Small imperfections can make the stencil more realistic when ink is added later because the stencil will look like rough-cut stone tiles.

3

To prime the floor mat, mix three pale colors with acrylic and latex paint. This will be the "grout" of the tiles you will paint with your stencils. Pour half a cup of flat white latex paint into each of three containers. Add a about two tablespoons of water to each container of paint. In one, add a little Burnt Sienna (about $\frac{1}{8}$ tablespoon). Add a little Yellow Ochre to the second and a combination of a tiny bit of Burnt Sienna and Phthalo Turquoise to the third. Stir the colors with craft sticks. With a foam brush, paint the colors on in random patches. Cover the entire canvas. Blend where the colors meet. Let it dry thoroughly.

4

Now you're ready to stencil. Here the corner stencils define where the border stencils go, the border stencils define where the little squares go, and all of that defines the middle. Pour about a quarter cup of white latex paint onto three Styrofoam plates. Add acrylic paint to these to make three colors, darker versions of what you made for the "grout." Spray a light coat of Spray Mount on the backs of all of the stencils to help adhere them to the floor mat. Using a natural sponge, dab color onto the floor mat through the stencil. Use all three colors without washing the sponge in between use—this will add richness to the tiles.

5

Carefully peel up the stencil. Be patient and allow each step to dry before you try to use the stencil again or stencil next to another tile. This will prevent paint from getting on the backs of your stencils and save you a lot of messy grief!

— **6 5** —

6

Continue stenciling around the border, allowing the paint to dry between each step.

7

As you can see in this design, the border defines the placement of the center design. When the whole floor mat is covered with tiles, allow it to dry thoroughly.

8

To make the tiles look three dimensional, pour some white latex paint into the three trays of paint to make the colors you just painted about 50% lighter. Place each stencil on the corresponding stenciled tile on the floor mat, shifting the stencil about an $\frac{1}{8}$ inch up and to the right. Lightly sponge the lighter paint onto the floor mat through the stencil, letting some of the dark paint peek through for texture. Each new stencil should be placed the same way—$\frac{1}{8}$ inch up and to the right—to create the illusion of slightly raised tiles and their shadowed edges. Once thoroughly dry, seal it with three coats of Varathane. Follow the manufacturer's instructions regarding drying time.

The Finished Floor Mat

Visit createmixedmedia.com/stencilcraft to access a bonus demonstration.

HOBBY BOXES

Painting a wooden box just scratches the surface of the three-dimensional things you can stencil. Unfinished wood furniture, street finds, wooden trays, table tops and bed headboards make wonderful surfaces to stencil and design to add richness to your home.

The design for the box in the following demonstration was inspired by the tile designs from the floor of the Basilica of di San Marco in Venice. You can find more interesting dimensional tile designs by searching "tromp l'oeil tile designs" on the Internet.

Seaside Treasures Box, Acrylic on Wooden Hobby Box
This hobby box was painted with a blend of acrylic colors. I cut out abstracted shells, fish, birds and other shapes from large Avery stickers and placed them evenly over the surface of the box. (You can also use stickers already in shapes instead of cutting your own.) I painted over the stencils with a natural sponge and Golden Acrylics Bone Black. Once dry, I removed the stickers and sealed it with a coat of Varathane. Mod Podge Gloss would also work well as a sealant.

Lace Box, Acrylic on Wooden Slide-Top Box
Paper doilies and plastic lace work great as stencils. You can cut them apart and secure them to almost any surface with a little tape and use either a natural sponge or stencil brush to paint through them. This hobby box was painted with Golden Acrylics Titan Buff and Bone Black, then coated with Varathane to seal and protect the surface. You could also use Mod Podge Gloss for this.

PAINT A HOBBY BOX

A wooden box from a craft supply store makes a wonderful surface to show off a fool-the-eye tile design. This project does take some careful planning and measuring, but the results are worth it. The stencil for printing all of the parts of the tile design on the top of the box is the same. The trick is cutting the stencil precisely, allowing each step to dry thoroughly (again, patience is required), and mixing the four values of gray-brown to create the illusion of depth. You might have to do a few samples on a piece of paper to get the value pattern just right.

MATERIALS

1" (25mm) chip brush

acrylic paint

craft knife, stencil burner or scissors (depending on the complexity of your design)

frosted or matte Mylar or clear acetate

latex paint (flat white)

masking tape

medium-weight drawing paper

Mod Podge Gloss

pencil

Sharpie marker (fine point)

stencil brush

wooden box

1

After you design and cut your stencil, prime the surface of the box with a base coat of acrylic paint. In this case, I used two pale colors: a little latex flat white paint mixed with Burnt Sienna, and another container of flat white latex mixed with Yellow Ochre, blended together with a chip brush.

— **69** —

2

Once the primed surface is dry, use a pencil to lightly mark the surface of the box with a grid pattern.

3

In four small containers, mix four different values of brown-gray acrylic using Raw Umber, black, white and a little Yellow Ochre. You will have to study the design you see here and paint a couple of sample designs on a separate piece of paper to get the illusion just right. Use a stencil brush to paint the darkest color first. Let it dry. Turn the stencil 45 degrees clockwise and paint the next lighter value of gray. Let it dry. Turn the stencil clockwise 180 degrees, paint the next lightest gray and so on until the design is complete.

— **70** —

4

Use masking tape to mark out a smaller grid pattern on the sides of the box. Paint all shades of gray with a stencil brush in a random pattern. Allow to dry completely. Carefully peel away the tape to reveal the finished design. Apply a coat of Mod Podge Gloss to seal the surface.

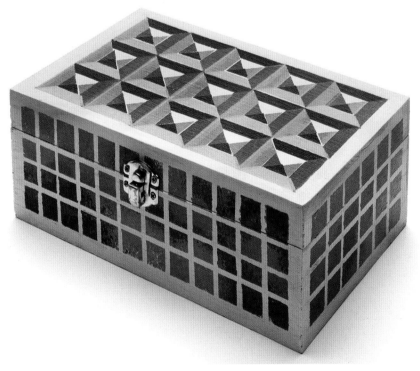

The Finished Hobby Box

Visit createmixedmedia.com/stencilcraft to access a bonus demonstration.

GREETING CARDS AND ENVELOPES
Acrylic and Colorbox stamp pad ink
on various papers

STENCILS FOR PAPER

04

I was standing in our local drugstore in the card section trying to pick out the "just right" card to send to a friend in need of congratulations. An artist friend spotted me there and asked, aghast, "What are YOU doing buying cards?" I slunk out—she was right. With maybe two hundred stencils stored in my stencil library and plenty of scraps of beautiful medium-weight drawing and decorative paper, why *was* I settling for the not-that-great best the drugstore could offer me for three dollars when I could print the perfect card myself?

The more stencils you cut for various projects, the more variety you have for card printing. You can design a different stencil each year to print holiday cards and package and sell cards at the holidays, too. In this chapter we will use stencils to design and print business cards and to recycle and glamorize brown paper for use as wrapping paper.

As you cut more stencils and build your stencil library, you will find more paper goods to personalize with them: bookmarks, book covers, hand-sewn sketchbooks to tuck into an envelope as a little gift, folders, organizers, calendars, even a blotter for your desk. If you walk around your local office supply store, you will collect even more ideas for paper goods to print.

— 73 —

GREETING CARDS

Blank cards are available for purchase at most art supply stores and some office supply stores. Strathmore makes a variety of sizes and paper types suitable for printing, some with a bright colored edge on the deckle. I always have bits and pieces of paper in my studio: middle-weight drawing paper, printmaking papers, medium-weight gampi, Canson papers in different colors. I bet you do, too.

You can buy card-shaped envelopes at office supply or stationery stores and cut your various scraps to fit. I usually make a template from a piece of regular computer paper that fits into the envelope I have purchased, making sure that it does not fit too snugly. I then use this template to set up my tabletop guillotine cutter to trim up several pieces at one time. You can tear paper for cards to make a pretty edge and print on the envelopes, too!

Never Buy Cards Again!
In a single afternoon you could cut a stencil, mix colors and print several cards with matching envelopes. When you cut stencils from acetate or Mylar and store them carefully, they can last for years. You can use these stencils from your stencil library to print greeting cards, thank-you notes, announcements and invitations. You may never have to shop at a card store again!

STATIONERY

Many people reading this book have a crafting business or are thinking of starting one (perhaps to sell hand-stenciled greeting cards?). You can design a logo stencil to personalize your craft business stationery: invoices, stationery, business cards and postcards announcing your next craft show. You could even cut the logo stencil in various sizes and print a canvas apron with it to wear when you teach classes, T-shirts for you and your sales helpers at craft shows, gift bags for your merchandise and canvas totes to thank your big buyers.

There is something about hand-printed postcards and business cards that tend to get saved instead of tossed out. The texture of the printed surface and the whimsy of a design encourage potential customers to hang on to these things, maybe even pinning them to a bulletin board to enjoy—and remind them of your wares.

For this project I printed out all the contact information onto the stationery pieces on my computer printer, leaving room for the stenciled logo. As obvious as it may seem, be sure to include your name, business name, telephone number, email address, URL if you have one and your mailing address on your business stationery. Print out postcards and business cards on card stock. Print stationery on a high-quality, high rag content paper. However, not all printers will accept paper that is not designed to be used in them. I can't recommend experimenting with your printer unless you are very brave or very desperate: I found out that mine would not take printmaking paper late one night when the ink-jet card stock I had purchased kept getting stuck, the stores were all closed, and I really needed to print something on a heavier weight paper.

Ink Works Best for Stationery
Acrylic is great for printing greeting cards as the thicker paper holds up to the thickness of the paint. Stamp pad ink works best for printing stationery as the ink adds a negligible weight to the finer weight paper.

Visit createmixedmedia.com/stencilcraft to access a bonus demonstration.

PRINT BUSINESS CARDS

Follow the steps to print your own unique business cards.

MATERIALS

bone folder

Colorbox Fluid Chalk Petal Point
pastel ink pad

foil sheet

frosted or matte Mylar or clear
acetate

Jones Tones foil glue

masking tape

pencil

Sharpie marker (fine point)

stencil burner

tracing paper

various stationery pieces such
as business cards and postcards
printed on card stock

1

Design and cut your stencil. Cutting the delicate detail on stencils to be used for stationery is most certainly a job for a stencil burner!

2

Use a Colorbox Fluid Chalk Petal Point pastel ink pad to stamp over the stencil design onto the card.

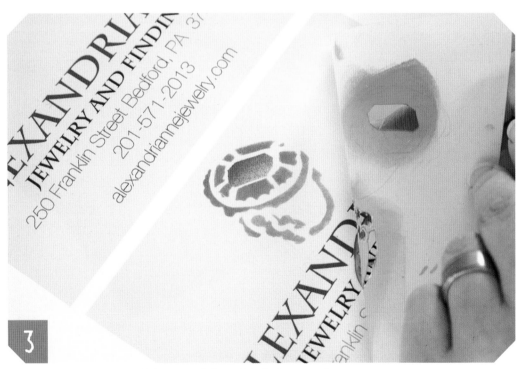

3

Allow it to dry and then carefully pel back the stencil to reveal the first layer.

Visit createmixedmedia.com/stencilcraft to access a bonus demonstration.

4

To add a little sparkle to the stencil, you can draw on it with Jones Tones Foil Glue.

5

Allow the glue to dry thoroughly. It will still be sticky, but clear and not milky. Place a small piece of pressure sensitive foil on the glue, shiny side up, and use a bone folder or the bowl-side of a teaspoon to gently burnish the foil onto the glue.

6

Carefully peel back the foil to reveal the finished design.

The Finished Business Cards

Visit createmixedmedia.com/stencilcraft to access a bonus demonstration.

GIFT WRAP

Every holiday that involves unwrapping gifts has always made me cringe—not because of the gifts inside the packages, but because of the amount of gift wrap that gets thrown away—sometimes only moments after the gift has been unwrapped.

Since I began printing my own gift wrap, I've found that recipients tend to unwrap my gifts to them more carefully as well as save the paper. Perhaps they are just waiting to toss it when they get home, but I'd like to think that they might be saving it to reuse. I hope so anyway!

You can also stencil-print gift bags with handles that can be reused multiple times, or take recycling to an even higher level by printing cloth gift bags that can be reused for years.

Brown Paper Packages Tied Up With String
You can buy craft paper in rolls at office supply stores. You can also cut apart brown grocery bags, iron them flat and print on the plain side. This way, you can print gorgeous individualized wrapping paper and feel cheerful about reusing and recycling.

DESIGN WRAPPING PAPER

Follow the steps to design and print this sun, moon and stars wrapping paper. This paper would be good for a variety of occasions, but you can design specific holiday theme papers with ornaments or snowflakes, hearts or numbers and birthday candles.

MATERIALS

½" (13mm) bright brush or a small stencil brush

acrylic paint or Colorbox Fluid Chalk Petal Point pastel ink pad

brown craft paper

craft knife, stencil burner or scissors (depending on the complexity of your design)

frosted or matte Mylar or clear acetate

masking tape

pencil

Sharpie marker (fine point)

tracing paper

water

Sketch out your designs for a sun, moon and a star. If you want the sun to have a face, you either have to build it into one stencil with bridges, like this one, or cut a second stencil in which you cut eyes, a nose and a mouth. The sideways moon is a little easier. After you are satisfied with your design, lay a piece of stencil material on top and tape it to your design. With a fine-point Sharpie, trace what you are going to cut out.

Cut the stencil. I cut this one with a craft knife on a self-healing cutting mat. See how the sun is subdivided to add the facial detail? That is just one way to do it—there are many other ways to design in the features. Cut out the moon and a star or two as well.

I painted this wrapping paper with Jacquard Lumiere paint because I wanted the metallic and pearlescent qualities of this line, but any acrylic paint or stamp pad ink works for wrapping paper. Do not use Spray Mount on the back of these stencils because the tack can pull up the fibers of the brown paper when you remove the stencil. Use a stencil brush to apply paint to the craft paper. Hold the stencil in place with your hand,

4

The blue stars add the final punctuation to this paper. You might also decide to spatter silver paint over the whole thing to add lots of little stars, or cut a smaller star stencil and add another color.

The Finished Gift Wrap

Visit createmixedmedia.com/stencilcraft to access a bonus demonstration.

DROSSELMEYER FLOCK
Ink and Gouache
on Rives BFK
22" × 30" (56cm × 76cm)

STENCILS FOR ART

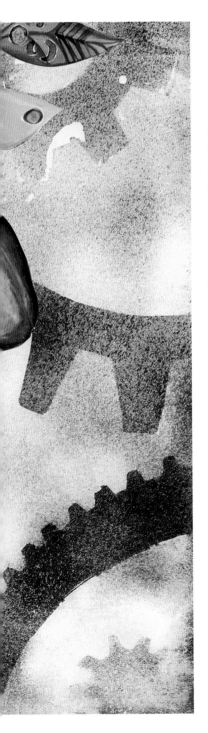

Stencils have a very particular look with their sharp edges and almost abstract graphic representation of light and shadow. Many artists use them in printmaking either as an end unto themselves or to spot in color on lithographs, etchings or photographs. The slightly raised edge of a stencil on top of another print adds dimension and texture to the printing surface.. The way the stencil is painted can vary from print to print, giving multiple prints in an edition a one-of-a-kind feel.

Pochoir plates were used in French fashion journals and pattern books in the early 1900s, around the time that Art Nouveau and Art Deco styles were popular. Stencils were made of thin sheets of copper or other metal, and colorists were employed to add the layered stencil images onto plates for the books. The insect motifs of E. A. Séguy's *Papillons* and *Insectes* are fabulous examples of this kind of printing.

Stencils have also long been used for portraiture. Silhouette portraits in the 1800s were actually cut paper. Today, stencil silhouttes can be printed on almost any surface. The stencil portrait of Barack Obama with the word *Hope* was seen everywhere during Obama's initial presidential campaign. The artist who created that image, Shepard Fairey, has made other bold portraits in stencils and also silkscreen, a similar medium. Other well-known artists such as Sonia Delaunay, Henri Matisse and Man Ray used stencils in their works as well.

You can also use stencils to print wall hangings that can be further drawn and stitched into. You can stencil into a sketchbook as a way to create a surface to bounce off of creatively when you are journaling. Stencils are quite versatile; they can make a painterly and textural surface or create crisp, graphic edges.

Visit createmixedmedia.com/stencilcraft to access a bonus demonstration.

PORTRAITS

Silhouette portraits were popular in the mid eighteenth century as an inexpensive alternative to having a fully painted portrait done. These portraits were typically a view from the side. Some were made with cut paper and some were a painted-in outline on paper occasionally highlighted with metallic paint.

Stencils lend themselves wonderfully to the silhouette portrait form. You can take a side-view photograph of a loved one and print it, trace around it onto a piece of stencil material, and make a silhouette stencil to print for a special occasion or gift.

Imagine two silhouettes facing each other for a wedding gift of decorative pillows, or framed silhouettes of grandchildren or beloved pets as birthday gifts. If you want more interior detail, pick a photograph that is high contrast with very bright lights and dark darks and use the darks to guide your creation of a stencil portrait.

Some of the most fantastic examples of stencil portraits come from the street artist world. You can do an Internet search for stencil portraits to see some examples of these.

Use Shadows When Creating One-Color Images

Trace around the shadows on a super high-contrast photo to make a dramatic one-color image. You can use this technique for a portrait of yourself, a friend or a family member or even a pet.

PRINTING AN EDITION

Editioning a print means that you do a set number of prints of the same image in exactly the same way, so the prints in an edition should be identical. Editions are great for gallery sales, art fairs and gift giving.

Images that are printed in an edition should be signed in a particular way. Edition prints are always signed on the paper below the print and in pencil. The edition number is shown on the left as a fraction (the top number being the specific print and the bottom number telling the total number of prints made). The name of the print, should it have one, goes in the middle. The date and artist's signature go on the right.

E=mc2, Edition of Ten
This famous figure makes a great stencil portrait. His hair in particular totally defines his head—there is no mistaking who this is!

In desperation for end-of-year teacher gifts for my son, I used this stencil, which was printed in acrylic on Rives BFK paper, to print tote bags to give away.

Visit createmixedmedia.com/stencilcraft to access a bonus demonstration.

PRINT A ONE-COLOR SELF PORTRAIT

Making the stencils for this portrait brought to mind the paint-by-number experiences from my childhood. The shadows and lights were separated out in a surprisingly abstract manner, and yet it usually all came together in a satisfying way. This self-portrait has only two colors, but you could make a stencil portrait in as many colors as a paint-by-number set, adding details and intricacy with each layer of color.

MATERIALS

black acrylic paint

computer

frosted or matte Mylar or clear acetate

masking tape

medium-weight printmaking or drawing paper

pencil

photo of yourself

printer

Sharpie marker (fine point)

stencil brush

stencil burner

tracing paper

EDITIONING AND PAPER PLACEMENT

If you are printing multiples for an edition, tape the top of the stencil to your work surface and tape a ruler or straight edge down so you have something to butt your printing paper against. This will ensure that your paper placement is the same every time.

1

Choose a dramatically lit picture of yourself and print it out as big as you can. It doesn't have to be high quality. Here I drew the back of my head in with a Sharpie directly onto the photograph as it was too low contrast to be seen when tracing in the next step.

2

Tape a piece of tracing paper over the photograph and start planning your stencil with a pencil. Draw around all the very lightest places and the dark places. There will be spots in the photo that are neither one nor the other—a medium tone—but you will have to decide whether or not they are black or white. Once you have decided what is black and what is white, commit to the lines by drawing over them with a Sharpie. You might want to color in some of the tracing to make sure it works.

3

With a fine-point Sharpie, trace the drawing onto a piece of stencil material, in this case matte Mylar. Since there are so many tiny details in this design, a stencil burner works great to cut it out.

— **89** —

Using a stencil brush and black acrylic, paint through the stencil onto the paper below.

Lift the stencil when the paint is not super wet yet not totally dry. If you wait until it is completely dry, the stencil can stick slightly and pull off some of the paper when you peel it off.

The Finished Self Portrait

Visit createmixedmedia.com/stencilcraft to access a bonus demonstration.

PRINT A TWO-COLOR PORTRAIT

Famous figures from history could make a really fun series of portraits. Albert Einstein, Abraham Lincoln, Thomas Jefferson, Marilyn Monroe, Maya Angelou, Alfred Hitchcock—any of these subjects would make distinctive stencil portraits.

MATERIALS

acrylic paint

bright light source (such as a flash-light)

frosted or matte Mylar or clear acetate

glass panel

pencil

masking tape

medium-weight printmaking or drawing paper

printer

reference photo

ruler

Sharpie marker (fine point)

stencil brush

stencil burner

tracing paper

1 For this portrait, I found an image in the public domain online. I took it to a copy shop and had it printed onto 11" × 17" (28cm × 43cm) paper. When doing the one-color portrait, you probably noticed there was more than just one shade of darkness. In a two color portrait, you can make that intermediate shade another stencil layer and another color.

— **92** —

2

When printing more than one color on multiple prints, you need a system for ensuring the two colors line up the same way every time. Place cross marks on the photograph and the two stencils to line them up. To print, tape the top of your two stencils to the printing table so the cross marks line up with the stencil for the lighter color on the bottom. Cut your paper to size, allowing for a 3" (75cm) border all around the portrait. Cut a few more than your planned edition size to allow for imperfection. Slip a piece of this paper under the taped stencils. When you have the paper just where you want it, tape a ruler to the table at the upper left corner of the paper so that every subsequent piece of paper can be abutted there and be in the same place every time.

3

Print all the lighter colors first on all of the edition. Flip back both stencils and abut a piece of paper against the ruler. Flip down only the stencil for the lighter color. Use a stencil brush and the lighter color acrylic (in this case, red), to paint through the stencil.

— 93 —

Lift the stencil when the paint is not super wet yet not totally dry.
Repeat steps 3 and 4 for all of the edition. Allow this first step to dry
thoroughly before you print the second color. Untape the stencil for
the lighter color and set this aside.

Abut one of the prints with the lighter color against the ruler. Flip
the dark color stencil down. Make extra sure that your registration
marks worked and that the stencil for the second color is placed
properly over the first color. Use a stencil brush and the darker color
(in this case, blue) to paint through the stencil. To get the right balance between your colors and the white of the paper you'll have to
mix and test the colors a few times to get a balance that pleases you.

The Finished Two-Color Portrait

Visit createmixedmedia.com/stencilcraft to access a bonus demonstration.

AMALGAM COMPOSITIONS

As you grow your stencil library, the stencil images will tend to break into categories that reflect your interests. You might have a lot of stars and planets, brocades and paisleys or abstract textures. In my library I have flowers and foliage, lots of woodland creatures, landscape edges (with silhouettes of buildings and trees), as well as sea creatures, coral, gears and birds.

You can use your collection of stencils to make an amalgam composition—a blend of individual images and textures to make one cohesive composition. As you figure out your composition, pay special attention to value pattern—the movement of dark and light across the paper. Some things won't make visual sense right away, so step back a few times while you are working and take your time figuring out what the next step should be.

DROSSELMEYER FLOCK
This picture is composed of an amalgam of different stencils from my stencil library and the gears from painting the clockwork lining of Drosselmeyer's cape from *A Nutcracker*. I placed the stencils and sprayed white gouache thinned to the consistency of half-and-half milk. Once dry, I painted India ink over the page, let it dry and washed the paper under water. The gouache dissolved leaving only the ink. The colored element is not a stencil, but was painted into the stenciled foreground.

CREATE AN AMALGAM COMPOSITION

In the composition for this demonstration, I combined flowers, foliage, branches and rural landscape edges to create a meadow landscape. Gather like stencils in your collection and make an amalgam composition that is unified by theme—all your undersea stencils or all the astral ones. You could combine your stencils in strange ways—a rocket landing in a flowery field or crows flying through floating gears. The juxtaposition of unlike things might make for an interesting series of artwork. Or you can layer and layer stencils until their specificity is veiled, so the composition becomes almost totally abstract.

MATERIALS

black liquid acrylic paint

frosted or matte Mylar or clear acetate

masking tape

medium-weight printmaking or drawing paper

natural sponge

pencil

Preval sprayer and container

self-healing cutting mat

scissors

Sharpie marker (fine point)

stencil brush

variety of traditional and found stencils

waxed paper

Tape a 1" (2.5cm) margin around the paper. Collect all the stencils you have that might appear in a fairly traditional landscape and lay them out on your paper until you get a feel for the general composition. Remove all but the background ones. Secure the background stencils with a little masking tape. If you have stencils with small margins that you're planning to spray, you might need to add to the margins by taping waxed paper to the edges of the stencils.

Spray black acrylic mixed with water (about 1:1) over the stencils.

While the paint is wet, brush off the stencil here and there with a stencil brush to add depth and a cloudy feel.

Place the mid ground stencil elements and tape them in place as needed. Spray the 1:1 mix of black acrylic and water over the midground stencils. Then place the foreground stencils (in this case weeds, grasses, a plastic branch of silk buds, a tree branch and a masking-tape trunk) and spray paint across them.

For detail in the foreground, dip into your collection of detail stencils to add elements such as berries, buds, flowers or dragonflies with black acrylic.

— **99** —

Step back to evaluate what you've done so far. In this case, I thought the just-black details looked too stark against the softer sprayed ground. On a palette, I mixed a couple of grays (one medium and one very light) and added lighter flowers and berries in among and on top of the black elements I printed.

Refine the details. I took off the big dead tree on the left and used that branch stencil to add more branches behind the tree and on the right of the composition. Some of this is based just on instinct. What looks good? When do I stop? Your piece will likely go through an "ugly" stage like mine did when it had the stark black elements and none of the gray printing. Relax, let things dry, step back and look. Don't panic if it doesn't look magically right through the whole process. Trust your instincts and have fun!

The Finished Piece

Visit createmixedmedia.com/stencilcraft to access a bonus demonstration.

GALLERY

WINTER LEAF
Gouache and India Ink on paper
7" × 11" (18cm × 28cm)

JUNGLE FERNS
Dye paint and batik on nylon
16"× 16" (41cm × 41cm)

Visit createmixedmedia.com/stencilcraft to access a bonus demonstration.

HUMMINGBIRD
Gouache and India Ink on paper
18" × 24" (46cm × 61cm)

Visit createmixedmedia.com/stencilcraft to access a bonus demonstration.

TRAVELING MINSTREL
From a series of stencil prints, *Call Down the Moon*
Gouache and acrylic on paper
13" × 15" (33cm × 38cm)

PIPING FOR THE HORSES
From a series of stencil prints, *Call Down the Moon*
Acrylic on paper
13" × 15" (33cm × 38cm)

THE COW TO JUMP
From a series of stencil prints, *Call Down the Moon*
Gouache and acrylic on paper
13"× 15" (33cm × 38cm)

RABBIT
From a series of stencil prints, *Call Down the Moon*
Gouache and acrylic on paper
13" × 15" (33cm × 38cm)

Visit createmixedmedia.com/stencilcraft to access a bonus demonstration.

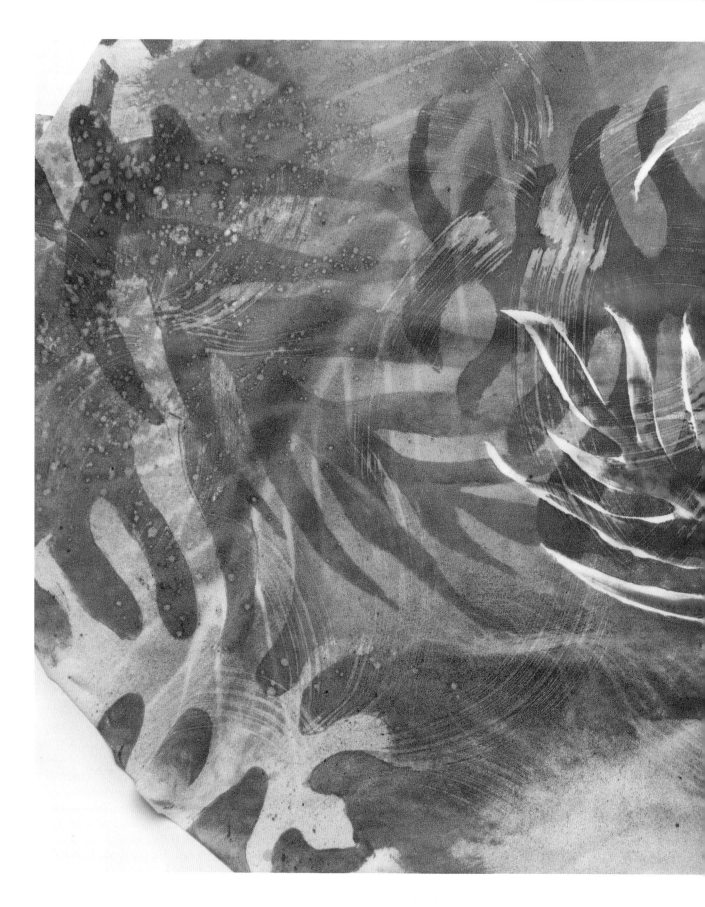

COSTUME SAMPLE
Silk paint and wax resist on stretch nylon 18"
× 24" (46cm × 61cm)

Visit createmixedmedia.com/stencilcraft to access a bonus demonstration.

ANGEL

From a series of prints, *Eulogy*
Acrylic on paper
13" × 15" (33cm × 38cm)

EULOGY QUILT
From a series of prints, *Eulogy*
Acrylic on paper
13" × 15" (33cm × 38cm)

Visit createmixedmedia.com/stencilcraft to access a bonus demonstration.

1/10 $E = MC^2$ M.A. Plot
2014

E = MC 2
Acrylic on paper, edition of 10
15" × 18" (38cm × 46cm)

OTIS
Acrylic on paper
15" × 18" (38cm × 46cm)

Visit createmixedmedia.com/stencilcraft to access a bonus demonstration.

HUMMINGBIRD 2
Gouache and India Ink on paper
9" × 11" (23cm × 28cm)

PAINTED SCARF
Dye paint on china silk
10" × 45" (25cm × 114cm)

Visit createmixedmedia.com/stencilcraft to access a bonus demonstration.

SKETCHBOOK PAGES
Gouache and India Ink on paper
8" × 24" (21cm × 60cm)

Visit createmixedmedia.com/stencilcraft to access a bonus demonstration.

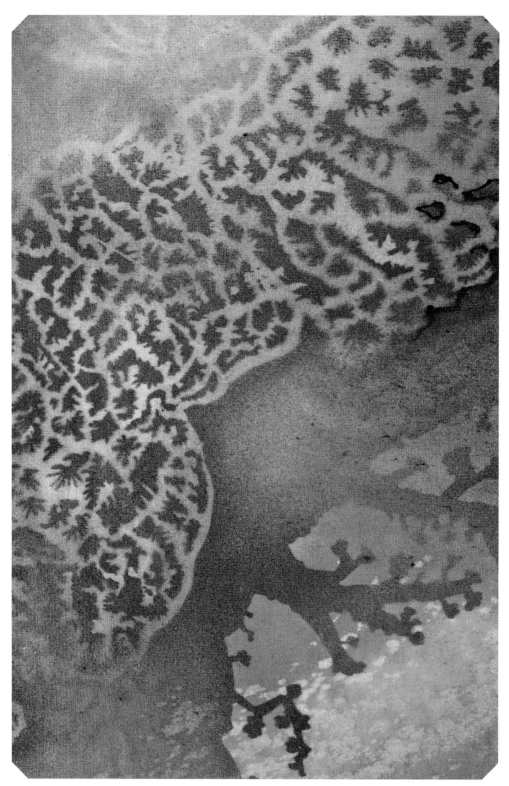

EULOGY QUILT
Silk paint and wax resist on stretch nylon
18" × 24" (46cm × 61cm)

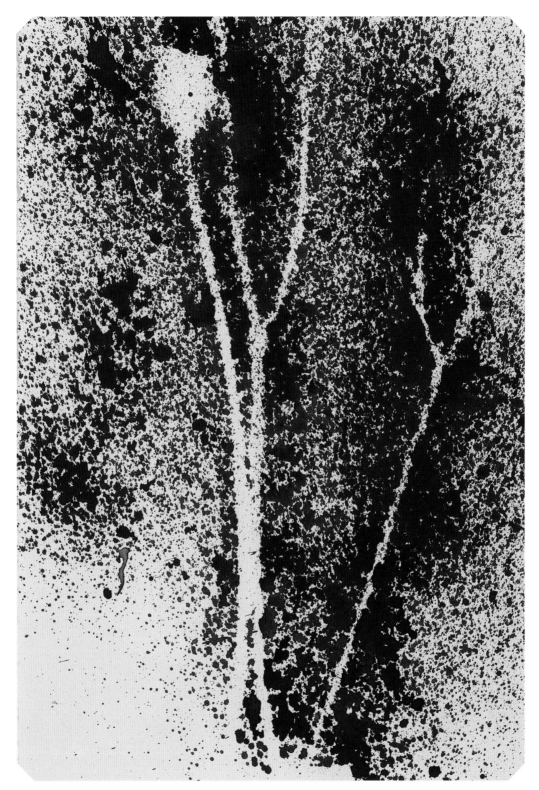

BRANCHES
Gouache and India Ink on paper
7" × 11" (18cm × 28cm)

Visit createmixedmedia.com/stencilcraft to access a bonus demonstration.

UNTITLED
Gouache and India Ink on paper
22" × 30" (56cm × 76cm)

Visit createmixedmedia.com/stencilcraft to access a bonus demonstration.

FURTHER READING

Stencil Girl: Mixed Media Techniques for Making and Using Stencils
Mary Beth Shaw
North Light Books, 2013
Mary Beth Shaw shows how to use stencils in combination with other art and mark-making techniques for unique effects.

Fabric Surface Design: Painting, Stamping, Rubbing, Stenciling, Silk Screening, Resists
Cheryl Rezendes
Storey Publishing, LLC, 2013
An encyclopedia for the home fabric painter, including stencil techniques.

Printing on Fabric: Techniques with Screens, Stencils, Inks and Dyes
Jen Swearington
Lark Crafts, 2013
A stylish book of mark-making on fabric including dye baths, bleach, resists.

Lotta Jansdotter Stencils: Decorate Your Walls, Furniture, Fabric, and More
Lotta Jansdotter
Chronicle Books, 2010
This book shows good stenciling projects, printing on textiles, wallpaper, walls.

Lotta Prints: How to Print with Anything, from Potatoes to Linoleum
Lotta Jansdotter and Jenny Hallengren
Chronicle Books, 2008

Printing By Hand: A Modern Guide to Printing with Handmade Stamps, Stencils and Silk Screens
Lena Corwin
Stewart, Tabori and Chang, 2008
This book shows printing of various kinds from a textile designer's perspective.

Stencil 101
Ed Roth
Chronicle Books, 2008
A portfolio of reusable stencils from urban-hip designs to birds and branches. There is a how-to booklet included with the stencils.

Stencil 201
Ed Roth
Chronicle Books, 2011
More reusable stencils from Ed Roth including retro-hip designs, and some abstract designs. There is a how-to booklet included with the stencils.

Stencil Nation
Manic D. Press, Inc., 2008
Russell Howze
Street art and graffiti.

The Street Art Stencil Book
On Studio
Laurence King Publishers, 2010
A portfolio of stencils printed on perforated card stock, designed by the artists of On Studio.

Street Logos
Tristan Manco
Thames & Hudson, Inc., 2004
21st Century graffiti art, including some exciting and innovative stencil designs.

Wall and Piece
Banksy
Random House, UK, 2007
The street art of the prolific and anonymous Banksy.

Receive bonus content when you sign up for our free newsletter at createmixedmedia.com.

INDEX

Other fine North Light Books are available from your favorite bookstore, art supply store or online supplier. Visit our website at fwcommunity.com.

19 18 17 16 15   5 4 3 2 1

a content + ecommerce company

DISTRIBUTED IN CANADA BY FRASER DIRECT
100 Armstrong Avenue
Georgetown, ON, Canada L7G 5S4
Tel: (905) 877-4411

DISTRIBUTED IN THE U.K. AND EUROPE
BY F&W MEDIA INTERNATIONAL LTD
Brunel House, Forde Close, Newton Abbot, TQ12 4PU, UK
Tel: (+44) 1626 323200, Fax: (+44) 1626 323319
Email: enquiries@fwmedia.com

DISTRIBUTED IN AUSTRALIA BY CAPRICORN LINK
P.O. Box 704, S. Windsor NSW, 2756 Australia
Tel: (02) 4560-1600; Fax: (02) 4577 5288
Email: books@capricornlink.com.au

ISBN 13: 9781440340116

Edited by Christina Richards
Designed by Elyse Schwanke
Production coordinated by Jennifer Bass

ABOUT THE AUTHOR

Margaret Peot has been painting and dyeing costumes at Parsons-Meares, LTD for more than twenty years for Broadway theater (*Aladdin, Spiderman: Turn Off the Dark, The Lion King, Wicked, Shrek The Musical, Spamalot* and hundred of other projects), dance (San Francisco Ballet's *The Nutcracker, Pilobolus*), television, film (*Bram Stoker's Dracula*) and circus (Ringling Bros. and Barnum and Bailey and The Big Apple Circus). She is a member of United Scenic Artists, and has guest-taught costume painting at Tisch School of the Arts at New York University, University of North Carolina, Brigham Young University, and the USITT-SE conference.

Margaret is also a writer. She is the author of *The Successful Artist's Career Guide: Finding Your Way in the Business of Art*, published by North Light Books, containing interviews with other artists, personal anecdotes, worksheets and practical advice for making a living as a visual artist. Her book *Make Your Mark: Explore Your Creativity and Discover Your Inner Artist* (Chronicle Books) contains no-fail, no-drawing-necessary techniques designed to jump-start creativity. *Make Your Mark* made Library Journal's Best How-To Books list of 2004.

Her book for kids, *Inkblot: Drip, Splat and Squish Your Way to Creativity*, published by Boyds Mills Press, received a starred review in *School Library Journal*, was awarded a Eureka! Silver Medal for non-fiction children's books, and is on the Orbis Pictus Recommended Books list for 2012.

Margaret is currently working on her first illustrated picture book, *Crow Made a Friend*, for Holiday House.

ACKNOWLEDGEMENTS

Every book project is the result of the tireless efforts of many. I would like to thank my wonderful editor, Christina Richards, photographer Christine Polomsky, as well as Beth Erikson and book designer Elyse Schwanke. Thanks to my terrific agent, Anna Olswanger. Additionally, big thanks to Sue Seitner, Skip Wachsberger, Gary Finkel, Lynn Pecktal, Frank Krenz, Virginia Clow, Michael J. Griffiths at Miami University, Michael and Jessica Carleton, Sally Ann Parsons and Parsons-Meares, Ltd., Hans, Kathie and Mark Peot and, as always, Daniel and Sam Levy.

Visit createmixedmedia.com/stencilcraft to access a bonus demonstration.

IDEAS. INSTRUCTION. INSPIRATION.

Receive FREE downloadable bonus materials when you sign up for our free newsletter at artistsnetwork.com/Newsletter_Thanks.

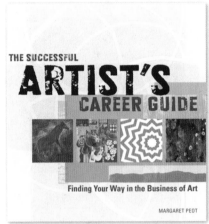

Find the latest issues of *The Artists Magazine* at your local newsstand or visit artistsnetwork.com.

These and other fine North Light products are available at your favorite art & craft retailer, bookstore or online supplier. Visit our websites at artistsnetwork.com and artistsnetwork.tv.

Follow North Light Books for the latest news, free wallpapers, free demos and chances to win FREE BOOKS!

VISIT ARTISTSNETWORK.COM & GET JEN'S NORTH LIGHT PICKS!

Get free step-by-step demonstrations along with reviews of the latest books, videos and downloads from Jennifer Lepore, Senior Editor and Online Education Manager at North Light Books.

GET INVOLVED

Learn from the experts. Join the conversation on